THE DEVIL CRUISES
PACIFIC COAST HIGHWAY

THE DEVIL CRUISES
PACIFIC COAST HIGHWAY

Poems by

Katherine Williams

© 2023 Katherine Williams. All rights reserved.
This material may not be reproduced in any form, published,
reprinted, recorded, performed, broadcast,
rewritten or redistributed without
the explicit permission of Katherine Williams.
All such actions are strictly prohibited by law.

Cover design by Shay Culligan
Cover Image: *Blood Lines,* acrylic, by Gaston Locklear

ISBN: 978-1-63980-335-4

Kelsay Books
502 South 1040 East, A-119
American Fork, Utah 84003
Kelsaybooks.com

for Richard

Acknowledgments

The author thanks Richard Garcia, the Long Table Poets, Susan Terris, and April Ossmann for significant feedback and edits, and the following print, online, and broadside publishers for making public some version of these poems:

Anthologies

Blue Arc West: An Anthology of California Poets: "After Shadows and Silence"

City of the Big Shoulders: An Anthology of Chicago Poetry: "Blueaille"

Java Monkey Speaks: A Poetry Anthology: "Amor Prohibido"

Kakalak: An Anthology of Carolina Poets: "Pythia Barbara," "Zeitgeist"

Mischief, Caprice, and Other Poetic Strategies: "Dream Date"

Ripple Effect: "Moon Shell"

Seeking: Poets Respond to Jonathan Green: "Crossing"

Southern Poetry Anthology: South Carolina: "The Shot"

Periodicals

Diagram: "Its"

Ekphrastic Review: "On the Wing"

Moonday Poetry: "White Whisper"

New Verse News: "Kyoto Protocol"

Poemeleon: "The Devil Cruises PCH," "Jubilate Louie," "Orthodoxy"

The Poetry Society of South Carolina Yearbook: "Epithalamion," "More Beautiful in France"

Porter Gulch Review: "April Pacific," "The Drop"

Projector: "Termite Art"

qarrtsiluni: "A Poet Takes His Girl Dancing"

Rat's Ass Review: "Black, Oh How I Want You Black"

Really System: "Math 345: Geometry of Solids"

Spillway: "Lost Heart," "Migration"

Weekly Hubris: "Leave," "The Plumbing on Oak Street," "Pura Vida," "The Summer of Nothing Moves"

Wherewithal: "Ode on Red," "On Modernism"

Broadsides

Beyond Baroque Literary Art Center, Los Angeles: "You Won't Need a Ticket"

Contents

I. Not Miracle Enough

It's	15
Fall	16
Always	17
Zeitgeist	18
Monday—Colour of Water	19
In the Shadows	20
The Prussian Model	21
Alkahest	22
On Modernism	23
Comprehensive Midterm	25
Satellite Image	26
Lamentation	27
Kyoto Protocol	28
Sand, Glass, Moon	29
Wipeout	30
Three Questions	32
More Beautiful in France	33
Black, Oh How I Want You Black	34
This Library Does Not Lend	36
What is Danger?	37
A New Field Manual for Theoretical Engineers, 2nd Edition	38
As If	39
Epithalamion	41
White Whisper	42
Math 345: Geometry of Solids	43

II. Do No Harm

You Won't Need a Ticket	47
Red Side Blues	49
Three Martini	51

Killer King	52
Lafayette, I Have Returned	54
San Quintín Harbor	56
Equations	57
Amicable Pre-Hearing Brunch	58
The Drop	59
The Summer of Nothing Moves	60
Sonnet Comparing David Lehmans	62
Lost Heart	63
Blue Star of Prague	64
Spike	66
Termite Art	67
Amor Prohibido	68
After Shadows and Silence	69
Orthodoxy	70
Critique	71
The Plumbing on Oak Street	72
The Jezebel Retires	73
Dream Date	74

III. On the Wing

Migration	79
Moon Shell	80
April Pacific	81
The Devil Cruises PCH	82
God Devil Ghazal	84
Whisper, Ashes, Night	86
Ode on Red	87
The Red Terrance	88
Blueaille	89
Spectrophotometry	91
After Many Years Out West	92

Leave	93
Pythia Barbara	95
No-one	97
Pura Vida	98
Crossing	99
The Shot	100
Jubilate Louie	101
On the Wing	104
A Poet Takes His Girl Dancing	105
Four Different Kinds of Light	106

I.

Not Miracle Enough

It's

a thing so small
the shapeliest mind
can't fix its density.
It's the locus of conflict
between what we each think matters,
where intangible wave crashes
onto ephemeral beach.

Consensus says let it seize you.
Inhale its ravishing colors,
travel its shifting latitudes.
When its random symmetries converge,
let the impact be manifest.
It is the hour of the name,
the chiral shape of dark.

Fall

What seems like years we've sweltered, breathing steam.
Past molten sunsets, fireflies burn and fade;
cicadas and bullfrogs deafen stifling heat.
Luciferous microbes swarm-shine midnight waves.
Cloud-static blisters the water's flat grey skin.
And then one day the white sky wakes up blue,
blurred edges go sharp in cold anemic sun.
Up high, squawking ospreys cut clean through
astringent air. The woods are strewn with leaves.
The predawn stars are strewn with Leonids.
A rosy fragrance hits—my focus swerves
towards tea olive's icy kiss. Forget
magnolia's lavish, overheated bloom—
Forget that I have long forgotten you.

Always

for Pat Hiott-Mason

A queen always conceals a cutlass.
Damsels always drag daggers.
Sissies always sling scalpels.
A wench always wears a weapon.

A nun always infers a kirpan.
Bitches always brandish their blades.
This dowager always channels a hatchet.
Widows always wield their razors.

Sheilas always shift their shivs.
Your mistress always moves her machete.
A matron will always tote an omelet.
Lassies always support their saxons.

Spinsters always hear scimitars at a distance.
The baroness always broadcasts her bayonet.
Real broads are always bearing a bowie.
A Southern lady always carries a knife.

Zeitgeist

All that summer, when I could still drink sloe gin fizz
but Scotch was becoming my favorite, our misery
continued. John hung around in his usual flux,
demonstrating freedom by trying to screw
every girl I knew. I was reading Nabokov,
flirting with the idea of moving to Peru,
going to life-drawing classes, hoping the next
hurricane swell would be Best Ever. John's
idiot brothers were doing no better:
Jack dropped out, started writing his name J-a-q,
Steve almost got picked out of a lineup—
losers! And then John becomes a gigolo.
Maybe in a year I'll move to Berlin,
not Lima, I thought, and in the interim,
outfit myself for some lofty intellectual
pursuit like linguistics. John, I'd ask,
querulously, I'm planning my hajj,
remember me when I'm gone, would you? I
seem not to matter to you all that much.
To be honest, I'd have thought about taking
up snake-handling to relieve the ennui, if
vanity hadn't been a concern. Where
were our parents? Why, drunk! I've decided
xenophilia wasn't so bad. My sister's a mystic,
you dabble in opiates, everyone fears Beelzebub—
zeitgeist of the Seventies in South Carolina.

Monday—Colour of Water

after Max Ernst

One minute you're asleep, dreaming
cousins trying on tiered skirts over crinolines—
then the tide inundates your four-poster,
your lacquered vanity floating past as the current
drags you under by your nightdress.
But even as the heirloom piano takes on water,
you want to save it—even when it soothes,
Relax, have a bourbon. The water will recede
eventually. Mildew will not stain
your old dolls' faces, and the body
beneath the floorboards will at last be baptized.
The satin ribbons of your peignoir drift
in the olive-grey, clanking flood.
Your mind slows to a crawl. You float,
your vestigial gills gasping at cousins,
lace, all that argument with the piano—
the piano! You try to buoy it, make it breathe—
and as your piano fills, your lungs empty.

In the Shadows

A man groans and turns where he lies dreaming in the shadows.
What's pleasant by day can be menacing in the shadows.

Crossing wet grass, Day's red heels step on Night's blue shawl.
Two girls catch lightning bugs flashing in the shadows.

Silent lightning strobes eleventh-hour palmettos.
Taboo, nocturnal secrets foaming in the shadows.

The dark side of the moon is the wrong thing to call it.
Radio plays the Big Bang propagating in the shadows.

In the pavilion shaggers guzzle gin and tonic.
They wait for the air to stop shimmering in the shadows.

Ozone and thudding raindrops hail the cyclone.
Evacuees curse fluorescents buzzing in the shadows.

Is darkness a star's photons blocked by an object?
Trace the shards of sun the oaks are casting in the shadows.

Dusk smells of jessamine and mildew, syncopated birdcalls.
This crazy yearning It's engendering in the shadows.

The Prussian Model

Let's now review the most important things
in school: to read and count, obey, be more
and better, get in line, to stand and sing
the anthem, pledge the flag. If we forswore
the Prussian Model, would we then express
milk from the maple? Could we have the log
base twelve of blue, the algebra of yes?
Br'er Rabbit doesn't win this apologue.
Though butterflies spawn cyclones, and a sneeze
may launch The Bomb by accident, cologne
to us is only scent, and Edam only cheese.
In such good soil, such inbred seeds are sown!
What if he'd but escaped the tar, and run?
We never learned the words, but we can hum.

Alkahest

Some time around 'eighty, might be June
or August, summer O-Chem, panic-stress
of exams. Peroxide-colored gibbous moon
throws blue 3 a.m. shadows as I obsess
on mechanisms, formulas for snake
venom, naphthalene. I'd go for law, but moot
court's got nothing on the zincblende-cake
of salt-air on car hoods, Jim's fifty-eight beaut
rusting out from under our makeouts. Garbo
as Ninotchka, Bartok's Third, *Macbeth* all play
for my attention. How I envy the hobo,
focused on food and shelter every day.
Same process yields rock salt and rhinestone,
but memory? As solid as cologne.

On Modernism

from Wikipedia, "Thing Theory"

Chicken theory
is a branch of critical theory

focusing
on the role of chickens in literature

and culture.
It borrows from Heidegger's

distinction
between objects and chickens,

whereby
an object becomes a chicken

when it's
somehow made to stand

out against
the backdrop of the world in which

it exists.
Chicken theorists look

at the role
of chickens within literature,

and the fixation
on particular objects. Chicken theory

holds up
particularly well, as it applies

to the study
of modernism, due to the dictates

of modernist poets,
such as T. S. Eliot's famous notion

of the objective
correlative, or William Carlos Williams's

declaration
that there should be no ideas

but in chickens.

Comprehensive Midterm

5 (b) Paint four equations for a wave.
6) Plug in venom, dopamine or scotch
as variables in a Fibonacci
spiral. Explain in (8) how news delays

tornadoes. 9) What happens in a day?
10) How does Lola play pianissimo?
13) State how we know the things we know.
15) Describe how to make bottled fulgurite,

according to Arabian myth, from light.
In binary notation, improvise
16 (a) through (c). 17) Revise
your calculations of a pirouette

in three-quarter view and silhouette.
18) Prove fear and pride, and juxtapose
the two. Include the proof of Dante's prose.
19) What is an empty set? Elaborate.

Satellite Image

Pass Christian, Mississippi

Rain, there's such a thing as too much company.
She had no patience for fashion or idle chat.

Dog, how much longer can we tread water?
She grew trees from nothing but sand and sun.

House, your busted windows show blue sky.
Her laughter, bourbon laced with arsenic and dope.

Corpse, please just drift on by.
Camille hurricaned her first home clean away.

Wind, all night we've heard you howling.
Her last known address? Found on a sat-map,

Rita's eye socket staring into space.

Lamentation

> *But thou, O LORD, art a shield for me; my glory,*
> *and the lifter up of mine head.*
> —Psalms 3:3

Creeping thyme sweetening footprints,
bougainvillea flaming in walled sunlight,
loquat gold-ripening on ropy branches—
But Lo! new flies, beetles and moths, blights of root
and wilts of leaf, villains of opportunity.
Oleander, poison oak, mistletoe, nightshade,
hardly offend the invading horde.

Yet forest is to asphalt as water is to wine.
Even Pharaoh shall succumb
to the roots beneath the street, and become tree.
Behold! Brother Spinach shall have his teeth.
Rot to roses, not miracle enough?
Glory in abundance!
But will Something be the Lifter Up of mine head?

Kyoto Protocol

Even in Kyoto—
hearing the cuckoo's cry—
I long for Kyoto.
              —Basho

Even in August there is now wildfire.
In spring, rains will take what remains.
Kyoto calls us from bygone times.
Hearing Kyoto, everyone stops and turns.
The fires are a small state now.
Cuckoo's eggs roast in foreign nests.
Cry for help, cry for mercy.
I scan the river, a trickle on pavement.
Long ago we were warned.
For one hundred years we flew into the sun—
Kyoto, we did not stop and turn in time.

Sand, Glass, Moon

Sea of glass:
clear sapphire soaks fine sand
white as moon.

Sunset on rising moon
tints her go-cup of gin.
Toes sift cool sand.

Mind like whipping sand,
eyes shot through with moon,
heart of glass.

Sand dune kiss, glass
memory, sickening moon.

Wipeout

Ahead on a country road, spooked by a stray baseball,
a horse rears, and I go over the handlebars topsy-turvy.
Johnny and them visit my coma. At the phosphorous
quarry we go skinny-dipping. After that we butcher
Drayton Hall's lawn with frisbees—the Jazz Messengers
blasting from the van, homework just a hologram.

Near the Picasso at the Museum of Holography
in Paris, a brunette blows a kiss; a baseball
strikes a plate. A blue-nailed messenger
grazes the roof with his wings and topsy-turvies:
Dead from heroin in Canada, found behind the butcher's.
Rob could light his numbers in Spanish with a *fósforo*.

Catching sunlight, that deep green phosphate
quarry still laps at my skull like a hologram
in its tube of light. In memory I've butchered
those days of tall grass mown into a baseball
diamond, days at the swimming-hole—topsy-turvied
them into time wasted. Were I a bicycle messenger,

I'd be a different kind of messenger,
giving bankers valentines inked in phosphorous
by an unknown hand. Life deals in topsy-turvies:
one minute you ride your bike, the next a hologram
has trespassed your blackout, hands you a baseball
signed by the friend who no longer butchers

swine for a living, but, alone in Toronto, has butchered
his veins. His winged flightless messengers
invade my coma like flocks of baseballs
in batting cages, whacked senseless. Phosphorescent
waves blaze the midnight beach, head-high holograms
we surfed in our dreams, until topsy-turvy

we wiped out into adulthood: topsy-turvied
lives of waterplay and laughter butchered
into so many lifeless routines, loves of holographic
duration. The horse-thrown cyclist's message:
no sense keeping old frisbees, phosphorous
swimming-holes, leathers torn off baseballs.

Butcher, addict, banker, hologram,
messenger, all whirl in space on a mossy baseball,
a topsy-turvy coma studded with phosphorous.

Three Questions

Yo, Johnny—dude, did you get off?
Peering through the thick blue haze of a badly rolled joint
at the white line winding around that skinny Blue Ridge road
trading your usual breathless insults with the dude who survived
laughing in an explosion of sweet smoke and letting the cherry fall
you took the bait—and Death took you on the ride of your life
rolling your Mustang into the bare dogwoods
of St Valentine's night Johnny
rolling you right into the bony arms
of the champion of your solitude—
in the final adrenalin rush, Johnny, did you get high?

God, Janet, you were such a bitch! How bravely you twisted
against the choking corset of Southern womanhood,
painting them ugly-ass paintings and making the rent on your back—
I know our men out there are pretty conventional
but did you have to go kissing that tree?
Death lurks in the trees,
anyone can see him out there in the swamp lightning
but only the desperate see him beckoning in the headlights
offering the ultimate seduction in the warm primordial mud—
Janet, I need to know, was death a good fuck?

Oh, Bonnie, honey, you chased and flirted with Death so much—
dope, tequila, cigarettes, violent husbands and fast cars—
you never expected death to turn and notice you the way he did, no?
courting you long hard and steady with the confidence of
a true romeo that ultimately he would take you—
and now that you finally had his interest
he didn't seem so sexy anymore
and you resisted his force like a palm tree in a hurricane
until you became a bare stick
your lovely fronds and coconuts all gone—
and with death hotter than ever for a bride without vanity
did you finally marry for love, Bonnie darling, in the end?

More Beautiful in France

Women are more beautiful in France—it happens the second your plane enters French airspace. It is because Frenchmen believe each and every female is enchanting. In France we are lovely, working the crossword, brushing breadcrumbs from our chins, dashing out bedraggle-headed to grab the bus. Beguiling, as we choose among eggplants or peel the paper label off a Stella. In France, the homeliest woman can stop time. Even when we stink, Frenchmen think of premium aged Roquefort, the raw purple onions of spring, or the crumbling letters they still treasure from their first prostitute.

The sight of a solitary woman in a café engenders pity in the Frenchman's throat. He has no choice but sit next to her, ask her name, and whether she enjoys the films of Buñuel as much as he. She indulges his helpless chivalry, puts her textbook aside, smiles, offers him a croissant, and says, Not as much as those of Cocteau. And she says, What about those ravens that blackened the sky today while the steeple bells rang. And, We know how seashells echo rushing waves, but it must have been the haunting wail in the whelks of Crete that gave rise to Bel Canto. And, Pardon me, my kind monsieur, but I must be going.

The ache in his throat gets worse as he watches her rise, alone, and walk. He would offer to escort her to her rendezvous, but these are modern times.

Black, Oh How I Want You Black

Negro, que te quiero negro,
black and silky as the lingerie
biting my flesh under jeans and leather
as I wait for a taxi on this menacing corner,
black as this tattered suitcase,
this street with the light shot out.

Lunatic on the sidewalk wringing his hands out—
Negro, que te quiero negro.
Broken promises bust out of my suitcase;
our lies stick to my skin like nylon lingerie
in August. Painted myself into a corner
again, but my mind has seized on your leather.

What an erotic sound, a man undoing his leather
belt, that buckle hitting the floor turns me inside out.
I've been waiting forever for a taxi on this corner—
Negro, que te quiero negro.
Twenty bucks, twenty minutes' worth of lingerie,
twenty thousand vagrant miles rattle my suitcase.

How I want to live out of this suitcase,
no address but a carryall of worn-out leather . . .
After I've made it with you, I keep the lingerie
unwashed, breathe with you on my face till I pass out.
Negro, que te quiero negro.
Three times now that driver's passed this corner

looking to score. Paco was the dealer on my corner
in Paris . . . my room could have fit in this suitcase.
Negro, que te quiero negro.
In Paris, everything is silk or leather,
and when they wash their things out,
they hang them over the sill, the laciest lingerie

fluttering like leaves along cobblestones. Lingerie
to make a man forget his own name, see on every corner
women with nothing but lingerie under their clothes. Out
here, we shut our honeymoons in suitcases
and resentments tan our vows into leather.
Negro, que te quiero negro.

If a cab comes for me, at this corner with my suitcase
of ruined leather, I'm off for Paris—but if not,
I'm coming, in a mouthful of black lingerie, back to you.

This Library Does Not Lend

There were so many wigs in New
York then, street corners on fire
under pretzels and chestnuts, windows
giving onto blue-blooded helium.
Here I thrummed into apex and
the hard limp of cocaine.

Marbles and mannequins all over,
banners of Longo, Pollock, tin curls
grafted onto dark roots, the glassy lights
opening wide against my face, a Russian
taxista declaiming the death of Lennon.
In his rear view I shifted my itchy wig.

Just as autumn stepped into its urn
all the wigs of New York descended
on Alphabet City for the first ever
of whatever it was that was there.
In their cocktail gowns and wigs
several angels shivered in the dirt.

Storeys above a vacant lot car-horns shifted
pixilating from red to green to yellow
through a window spattered in sooty rain,
I lay in dingy rumpled sheets,
tongue rank with another beginner angel,
my pillow a t-shirt stuffed with wigs.

They still test me, obsolete subway token,
crumbling copy of *The Village Voice*
with its annotated Free and Under Two Fifty,
ragged Cocteau double-feature ticket stub.
The wind down those tall avenues.
All those wigs trending toward the clouds.

What is Danger?

Far from the beach, she sits on her board, catching her breath. Sandy wax strafes her sunburnt skin.

A set arrives. Gone the battles over rent. No more O-chem final, which one killed her little sister, why Bobby left. Fuck it.

Just the shape of her hands as they knife clear water. Just aching traps and rhomboids. Just her sleek Challenger skimming the surface. Just breathe.

The first lip feathers as it thrusts forward and crashes. Letting it go, she feels afraid.

Some guy catches the second wave late, pearls. His board tombstones, the taut leash recoils. His fins are catapulted toward her, so she turns turtle. A giant section calves above her.

An iceberg of tiny bubbles fizzes her blistered skin. Her lungs burn. Her arms and legs hold tight, tight around her board.

A New Field Manual for Theoretical Engineers, 2nd Edition

After my chest was split open, and I was stitched
into a slant six engine with overhead cams,
I died anyway. Now, I run on hydrogen.
They gave my eyes to a Cambodian six year-old.

Water is the densest fluid but O, my brother,
Yeak Laom's lake once torched a mountain.
Cambodia, still more anhinga than engine,
is color-blind like me, its greens going grey.

The Cambodian girl who used to play
both hloy and sralai as well as any nun,
now has lasik-perfected hazel eyes,
and weaves fuel cells out of rushes.

My body was once 97% water and 3% metal.
Now, it is a wave when not a particle.
So I ask you, O, my brother,
is time a waterfall, or is it a song?

As If

As if no accordions siren through Gare d'Austerlitz,
you ride off in search of *The Nostalgia
of the Infinite* alone—as if autumn in France
were not the sunny red daybeds of Matisse,
but a grey-brown Braque newspaper collage.
You rattle along, coughing into a ragged
two-franc copy of *Le Spleen de Paris,*
as if you could forget shining Jupiter Beach,
or the phosphate quarry's viridian waters.
As if you could do anything about it,
you despair the Vichy deportations,
the fading caves of Lascaux, your daddy's
passion for driving under the influence—
then, as if all Europe's clocks weren't ticking,
you wake on a vile Marseillaise waterfront
with a young Ocker in your sleeping bag
who takes your hand across the Pyrenees.
Straight off your library ladder, you dive
into his university of carpentry and goats,
as if you needed another degree.
As if he weren't singing in broad slang to you,
undoing your American laces in the dark,
you keep messing with your camera.
How could you have let him go at Calais,
that squalling and ungodly-frigid beach,
as if the only shells were those of the Allies
stuck unexploded in the ramparts?
You see now, how you torched on
for Nostalgia—her indiscriminate loves,
her trips to copy Raphael at the Louvre,
as if Raphael can be copied in bereavement.
So now you count bullet-holes
in this Normandy cliff as if you're not fifty,

advancing into moonlit Florida breakers
in shoes and socks, watching the driver
of a speeding Citroën curse as the last ferry
shoves off for Dover. As if you taste
those Florida breakers, not the magnum of Moët,
as if the Ocker with your fingers
in his mouth does not love you,
as if the red-painted caves of Lascaux
aren't fading down to grey no matter what.

Epithalamion

Cymbidiums in tidy nests of peat.
A Genoise in stacks, nasturtiums atop.
Men and maids upholstered in muted teal.

One mother stifles her lament;
the other pours another bourbon over mint.
One father sprang for a phaeton;
the other gives not one iota.

The bride gives her lips a coppery patina,
her nails get a fourth coat of paint;
she adjusts the temporary halo.

To the groom, slightly more man than animal,
all this fuss makes less sense than Latin;
he'd rather be installing laminate.

The oak under which they all met,
roots heaving, ants working at the pith,
feels its heavy branches going to peat.
Soon put to the lathe,
they'll smoke like paper, whine like metal.

White Whisper

mainsail reefed against violent wind-torn seas
aerated ice, sun-bleached driftwood
Maltese puppy teething on a high-lead doorsill
thunderheads smudged with burnt pine
window frames unhinging their shutters
a bird skull: air bounded by a force field
bridal gown whispering *untrue already*
song in an Indian key between F and F-sharp
blinding blaze of acetylene blowtorch
five-thousand-year-old femur
snowy beard of Saint Nicholas, patron of lowlifes
anemia, leukemia, hypoglycemia
ghost crab foraging empty sand
unkept secret
confessional amen
bleached-out shadows on nuclear walls
color of Chinese grief
breath frozen in a carpenter's moustache
fogbound full moon dulling the buoy-bell
warhorse of bloodied Mongol priestess
swell exploding into mountainous foam
cat feet ruffling a mirroring creek
percale sheets whispering *wrong person*
flashing ray of the lighthouse, sweep of the arc—
O blank page of defeat,
rise off the ground,
into summer's dead white sky.

Math 345: Geometry of Solids

We built this cairn as we keened,
flinty cairn, marking us across blind fog
above red fjords of solstice and equinox.
We fit stones together with our woolen hands.

We built this obelisk of haloes,
obelisk of petrified cosmic dust,
focusing waves of zodiacal light.
Like lead and fire, together we yield gold.

We built this parabola on ciphers,
parabola detecting music of the spheres,
faraway sulfurous ponds of biopoesis.
Together we throb across the continuum.

We built this fractal antenna on the wing,
tiny antenna receiving microwaves
through solar fountains and solar conjunction.
Together we whisper, *Is anyone out there?*

II.

Do No Harm

You Won't Need a Ticket

It's only 23 miles up.
All you do is rise beyond the muggy
evening and then fall into the desert
night. Rise above the live oaks
and loblollies, above the monarchs
and geese beating against the Gulf
Stream, above the feverish alluvial
vat, up into thunderhead, into ice.
You might have to bend your fingers
to steer between all the Boeings.
Your breath will crystallize
when you've reached your slow
dark above the blue dazzle.
Now, this is the only hard part:
you have to stay in place,
and not get stuck in geostationery orbit.
To pass the time, you can count
to fourteen thousand four-hundred,
or replay *The Decalogue* or all six
Bach Cello Suites, or maybe repeat
OK Computer or Psalm Twenty Three
or OM in your mind, and just float.
Or watch the once-majestic
Blue Ridge continue dissolving
into delta, naming the cities that pass
below as the Mississippi, Ozarks,
prairie, mesas, hoodoos, and the High
Sierras all turn towards sunrise.
Then clasp hands and dive
twenty-three miles, threading through contrails,
brushing the tops of sequoias making
their passage eastward. Drop down
through the weatherless signals

blasting from atop Mount Wilson, past T-shirted
skiers scraping Mt. Baldy. Let internet data
and monoxide fumes pass through
your body and, one toe bent to guide
yourself above the traffic of I-10,
you'll alight onto the sands of Venice,
not thirsty, not hungry, nor airport-weary,
but your mouth fizzing with stars.

Red Side Blues

Chaos rules the ER at full moon,
when the streetlights cast no shadow.
Homeless guy talking a blue streak—
Is he hearing voices? Only on Mondays?
Fine, if they don't say to kill someone. Crips and Bloods,
every night a bloodbath. Bloody blue blazes,

it's a simple question, sir, tell me—what in Blazes—
Never mind, get him up to psych. God do I hate the full moon.
Get restraints on that OD in three, do a blood
type and cross on the stab wound in five. See that shadow
on Six's chest x-ray, get a consult . . . Sunday to go, Monday
can't come soon enough. Check the red streak

up her leg in two. Run this up to micro, we need a streak
on four's throat—and good luck, place'll be ablaze
before those guys get a move on—Okay, Steve, see you Monday.
Where did all these gomers come from? Typical full moon,
women birthing on gurneys in the halls. Two interns to shadow
us from USC? Please, no more spoiled blue-blooded

brats, not tonight. Gunshotwoundtothehead, bloody
brain matter out of his left ear, no more lucky streak
for this banger. Full moon, black and blue shadows.
Next week I'm off, hello sax! Jazz at the Oliphant blazes
a different kind of hot on the full moon.
Whatcha think, another dead banger by ten? Monday

I can't forget the DMV. What else was on Monday?
Dammit the trach tube won't go in . . . is that blood
gas back yet? Folks, here's our next banger. Full moon
gang war, awesome . . . GSW leg, prisoner, face bloody—
Deputy, be nice to my patient, or get the fuck out
of my ER. Jean, take a look at the shadows

on this MRI. They always wait too late to bring their shadows
to the ER. Get a head CT on that prisoner. What else on Monday,
tax man? Chopper over the parking lot, searchlight blazing.
That one with his face bashed in, sleeve all bloody—
he goes to pediatrics. Never saw such a killing streak.
Thank God it's just once in a blue moon.

Sunup—tall shadows, dewy windshields, round smoggy moon.
Fresh air blazes my eyes into bloody coals. Nobody's
keyed my ride! Bed soon . . . Monday's two streaks of dawn away.

Three Martini

three martini like roadblock
makeup like mouse in shoebox

bed like laryngitis
dream like dirty house

dog bark like ambulance
alarm clock like water balloon

coffee like rusty pipes
shower like lucky strike

closet like trash truck
prius like dishrag

traffic like pipe bomb
office like paddy wagon

email like blackout
lunch like door painted shut

boss like fat deer tick
supermarket like Lo-Jack

neighborhood like barbed wire
driveway like term paper

news like loony bin
phone call like *you again*

sunset like mud streak
three martini like road block

Killer King

You can have the LAPD chopper circling overhead,
interrupting my poolside hibachi cookouts.

I'm taking my nightly jet-count
under the flight path, sipping straight tequila.

I'll keep the never-wearing of red or blue,
and the dazzling midnight landings of life-flights.

For you, the gorgeous, half-psychotic Manager, rude
to everyone, but especially to *wives or whatever*.

You can keep the week on Kaua'i with Ken and Barbie,
that ghastly Sheraton luau they thought was so great;

the waves at Brennecke's and museum lei-making
are mine, the mask and snorkel, and my first mango.

Let's snap all our Blue Note records down the middle,
and the Hollywood Bowl subscription, and the skis.

I'm keeping the Spanish, and the French. You keep
the ER gurneys in free-fall during the Whittier Quake.

Mine forever, that haunting odor of shattered glass,
that old post-traumatic dive when the A/C kicks in.

My sister's diagnosis and ordeal never fade,
so I might as well keep them. You keep the lawyer

you paid to harass my vigil at Walter Reed.
And that plaid-suit accountant? Baby, he's all yours.

Oh, and in this poem, I'm not the gentleman
who let you take the cheap O'Keeffe and Merritt stove

I'll pay twelve hundred to replace. I'm keeping it,
and the never-heading-home on a nearly empty tank.

And though I'll pay for it the rest of my life, you keep
your lousy degree, your vow to do no harm.

Lafayette, I Have Returned

Moët explodes like a television tube
on Rennes Station's marble floor.
Same comestibles, four months solid:
plonk de plonk, fifty cents a kilo;
aging Camembert, weapons-grade;
a cobblestone of fresh brown bread.
Same hostel breakfast always, a deep bowl
of coffee and milk, steamy crackling pillows
of bread buttered with butter churned
yesterday, apricot or raspberry jam.
Showers so icy you gasp, shield yourself.
Knee-deep green fescues blanket rock cliffs
above still seas once dark with Celtic blood.
Windows framed in hand-tatted laces
reflect blue water, bare white masts,
dull chime of wind-battered spars.
Bundled up in the latest Parisian mode,
women settle the seawall like pigeons,
their speech a river rushing fast
over smooth black millstones, fingers
speed-knitting, eyes drilled into young
men kite-surfing the icy Channel.
A Gothic church, 12th-century,
its blitzed north transept replaced
with a steel-and-glass Bauhaus tower
set askew, rockets upward into grey sky.
Each town with its Stations of the Cross,
its altar, its stained-glass portraits
rendered by a famed ancestral prodigy.
Vertical streets convey parents and strollers
up past weavers and ceramicists.

Not only is every waiter surly, shopkeepers
pepper patrons with insults. Each town
with its war-dead names heaped in stone
under a bronze cockerel *pour la patrie.*
Party means drink all night—no excuses.
Drizzly morning at *Bar des Sports,* a man
raises his Bordeaux, asks, *Irlandaise, vous?*
Ah mais non, vous êtes Americaine! Six old
men leap from their stools at once, stand,
and salute: *Je me souviens de Normandie.*
I study the floor and toe at the mud I tracked in.

San Quintín Harbor

> *. . . the light gleams, and is gone.*
> —Matthew Arnold

She guides the aging Honda like a scalpel
along the bean field's edge, two wheel-ruts
ribboning a shallow cliff carved out
by the glimmering, now-tranquil bay.
He throws the tent down on a strip of beach,
a dinosaur's nest of wet stones stuck in sand.
They face the tent door open to the sea.
Deciding not to worry about *federales,*
he suns; she gathers driftwood, starts a fire.
He never learned to read the water;
she's been forced to read everything but.
She steams the mussels they clipped
this morning from a bed exposed at low tide.
They eat them with lime and salt, drink Coronas,
talk over the clack of eroding stones
about hospitals, about how verdant Baja
gets with irrigation, about someday sailing
to Sydney if it doesn't sink first.
They have not had sex in a year.
The stones shred their long purple shadows
as they wade in the sunset.
Only seaweed and driftwood lace the beach,
shells long since pulverized to sand. Pounding
each other smooth in the high-tide shallows,
loose stones make a thudding sound.
Venus casts a dark reflection on the horizon.
No panacea, she murmurs to herself, scanning
the brocade of stars beaded with darkling sky.
Throughout the night, rogue dreams
wash their camp out to sea.
At last, slate-blue dawn . . . the tide is low.
The wind has stilled, the rose moon sinks,
the quiet stones glow like mangoes in the sun.

Equations

He syncopated his thoughts on every surface.
She spanned their auras with scientific rigor.

Who as a boy quantified each idolatry in the house.
Who as a girl never asked the color of bondage.

Who shrapneled his face with Chinese lightning.
Who held still as her silhouette dissolved.

His unorthodoxy, his lost elders, his wit.
Her pedigree, her catholic but hasty appetites.

His chapel of the cuttingest edge.
Her studio of jagged paradigms.

Their threshold, pristine with fault.
Their unregenerate laughter, their masks.

Her dessication, his consolidation.
His casuistry, her sacrifice.

Their seeing, striving to be blind.

Amicable Pre-Hearing Brunch

Let's let this shiny Aztec fetish be
the mussels left alive at San Quintín,
this knife, the knife we took them with, this green
and empty goblet represent the sea
we did not swim in, and the orange silk,
the school of red rock-cod we did not see;
the squeaky tabletop the all-night screech
of roosters we did not hear, the ring of milk
the moon, our only light. Let melted ice
stand for the tepid nuptials that denied
the abundant open life we tried
to undertake—a stopped clock, right twice.
The saucer amply holds our deepest vows,
the cup, the years that amplified our flaws.

The Drop

Hauling me out
to the impact zone,
one arm is lost
in the stunning cold,
the other poised to plunge.
In from the grey expanse
comes my leviathan.
Bathed in adrenalin,
I claw my way into
its murky green magnitude.
Standing weightless
and fluid, I rip a gash
down the face of time.
I nearly make the drop
and fall into the face—
but something's not right.
I've been held under
but not like this:
I never felt so turbulent,
then still.
The bottom-dwellers
want me home,
but I don't go well.
My burning lungs
flood with cold—
then with surrender,
easing me back in
to the Afterlife.
My bleached-out hair,
like my blueing fingers,
drifts with the current.
The last of my oxygen
flares up to the light.
My final thought:
I made it.

The Summer of Nothing Moves

It is the Summer of Star-Maps and Brad-Pitt-stories,
of *Can I go on a date while I'm out here please Auntie.*
Summer of Sister's-only-child-bursting-out-at-twelve.

It is the Summer of All-day-in-front-of-the-soaps,
Since you won't let me ride the bus to Hollywood.
I guess they don't teach the word *pimp* in parochial school.

*Honey—if I meet him and like him, and his parents bring him
to the movies and afterwards we all go home—then maybe.*
Summer of Last-year-we-played-Barbie-dolls-in-the-yard.

*Auntie, you don't have to do any of that, if he drives
his own car.* Summer of Honey-your-first-sexual-
experiences-should-be-with-someone-your-own-age.

Camping gear in the trunk, it's now the Summer of Kidnap.
Summer of Breakfast-outside-the-tent, of *I don't drink
tea with dirt in it.* Summer of Traffic-jam-L.A.-to-Vegas.

Summer of Buck-and-Doe-Road, fifty miles of jagged Mojave
stones, of *I don't see Indians anywhere.* Nothing moves
but my Japanese sedan, and heat rippling up from the hood.

We rattle past one tour-bus, parked outside a makeshift casino.
Nothing moves but our wake of dust. Twenty miles
until the South Rim. Summer of-Grand-Canyon-all-to-ourselves.

Halfway home, we will have a blowout. Summer of Michelin-
like-a-tuna-can-ripped-with-a-churchkey. I will teach
my sister's only child how to use a jack, how to loosen lugs.

She will pay close attention. In the Summer of Cell-phones-
haven't-been-invented-yet, I will not mention that, if our donut
spare shreds, we have a tent for shade, and three days of water.

But that hasn't happened yet. She's prattling about her choir
trip to France. I explain cell signaling cascades, basic surfing,
photosynthesis. Summer of Can-we-please-get-back-to-Brad-Pitt.

Tires intact so far, we push through acetylene heat out to the edge,
park the sedan, sit on a stone. Nothing moves before this great gash
in the Earth but the slow turning universe, our breathing bodies.

Sonnet Comparing David Lehmans

*Write a bouts-rimés on any W.H. Auden sonnet
and you'll have yourself a great poem.*
—David Lehman

Verizon bill—4k?! I nearly died,
seeing the total. This was taking safe
sex to extremes, conjuring breast-to-calf
on 1-900-GET-LAID. From outside
his room, I served eviction. Any doubt
he's at it still?
                Between romance and death
the poet ponders words, out on the heath
in his silk shirt, his ballpoint petered out
in mid-abecedarian, yes sad
about the war, but blissed-out in the House
of Lyric Moments.
                Time suspended in glad
imaginings, indulgence *sans* remorse
is all any of us wants in the course
of a day. About the bill, though, I'm still mad.

Lost Heart

Though she gets along fine without it, one day La Araña's heart arrives in a small Fedex box. It's supposed to be frozen, but the dry ice is long gone. The heart is warm and beginning to smell.

What's that sudden thumping in her ears? She remembers having had blood: she was in Graziela's kitchen in Rome slicing an eggplant, and sucked the gash. It had tasted rusty, or maybe green. Graziela's last words to her, *Verde, que te quiero verde.* —*Cold day in hell,* her retort.

Every time someone wants her, she loses heart. She imagines Graziela drinking absinthe on the balcony with Lorca and C.D., but La Araña can only wish, as she inhales the odor of the ripening muscle in the Fedex mailer, as Felix, her companion goat, browses the packaging.

The label, penned in Graziela's hand, is dated ten years into the future. Her heart will have begun to rot by the time it arrives, but maybe there is still time . . . her heart of garnet, of ashes, heart of light . . . La Araña scolds, *You've been at the books again, O Nimble Goat of Blank Verse.*

Bearing the box on her hip, she launches down the stairs in iambs, jolting the heart into synchronous beating. La Araña scolds, *Che fa,* Neapolitan for *what the hell.* The heart in the box keeps drumming, *As any she belied with false compare*—and, looking up from his poems, the pentametrical goat speaks: *Oh, Yeah.*

Blue Star of Prague

after Joseph Cornell

In Mexico, *conserjes*
do not like to rent rooms
to desperate women,
sand in their hair, twigs in their mouth,
ravening eyes gleaming,
the kind who go all over town at midnight
inquiring from desk to desk
whether their cash is acceptable—
Claro que no.

Until they happen upon the Estrella Azul de Praga,
a decrepit glory of crumbling stucco,
woodwork going to sponge—
never mind the buzzing fluorescent glare,
the bedbug mariachis, the stifling heat—
Refugio is manning the reception tonight.
The worst cases get the room with the picture
of a faded cupid over the bed, poling a boat
laden with sweet-nectared vines,
crossing a river of gentle wavelets.

Here a desperate woman can fall
into a desperate sleep
to a bad Western involving a bad gringo
with a bad gringo accent
who comes to her in a dream
and says that unless
she surrenders her virtues
the seagulls will be lost
—*I have only vices,* she says,
go ask a librarian—

and alone in a strange town
with light in her hands and wind for a name
such women wake up with
their feet already on the floor.
Refugio greets them with *café con canela,*
draws them a hot bath,
throws opens the creaking doors
onto a sunlit Avenida Revolución

Spike

Hardly a day goes by that I don't think of the spike in my head, I remark over coffee. You look at me as if I have a spike in my head—*Exactly.* I could yank it out . . . but I can't resist braiding it with pearls and satin for a night out. Working construction, I wrap it with a purple bandanna and stick pencils in, to complement the cleated boots. Before I got my spike, I was much shorter. Besides, turning my head gives a radio signal, and now I even get satellite internet. Where once I had nothing, now I own a tower. *Don't slurp your coffee,* you tell me. *Let it cool off.*

Termite Art

The Muse's gun aims at my nervous face.
Not gangland terminology again!
Can't we case the joint first? *Write,* she hisses.
The page stays blank under my crapped-out pen.
*Try using jargon or an action verb
to start each line,* she whispers, whisky breath
metallic on my shoulder. *I need bourbon,*
I mutter. The muzzle cuts my neck.
To fence, to fink, to finish? What the hell
do I know from Chicago Lightning? *Write.*
Pen scratches page. Her gun jabs deeper, *Tell
about the one they shot—in black and white,
a single take—*our sociopathic love
of lovers' crimes, the Muse's lust thereof.

Amor Prohibido

Was it the way the north wind gave voice
to palm timbales and gumtree cymbals,
salt spray bearing tortilla and fish-stink
up to our third rooftop music lesson,

or the way we went from shop to shop
on the field trip to San Ysidro
to catch a papier-mâché mermaid,
since they lose so much in translation,

or the ancient waitress at that tiki dive
on Hollywood Boulevard, expertly
lowering the torch so I wouldn't miss
the fine print on your halo in the dark,

or when Gypsies howled our lawless tango,
you wanting me green, my dead mother
whispering *Never give in,*
or the margarita kiss that ended all that?

After Shadows and Silence

whose eyes are the first espresso after customs
whose loins are stacks of firewood in winter
the one whose back is *Guernica* as it hung in exile
whose mind is an advancing hurricane
whose fingertips are the marimbas of Veracruz
whose tongue is a robe of silk crêpe de chine
the one whose spleen is Paris
whose ears are shiitake mushrooms in hoisin sauce
whose breath is autumn in Appalachia
whose toes are the *Moonlight Sonata*
whose chest is Vesuvius across the bay
whose shoulders are the rumor of armistice
whose gaze cascades the canyon between us
the one whose voice is perdition

Orthodoxy

if i am held breath fogging the night's glass
then you are a sequoia with coppery eyes
as the river overruns its muddy banks

if you are lost to the birds and fishes
then i am wind on the nape of your neck
as the rising tide erodes the petroglyphs

if i am a lunatic spelling the walls purple
then you are veins of garnet in a virgin rock-bed
as the south swell steals the sand

if you are a harvest of eyes and tongues
then i swallow mouthfuls of earth in secret
as black rain stabs the lagoon's bright skin

if i am a siren twisting in sleep
then you are the blind hand finding the prize
as the undertow churns up ruined shells

if you cannot rest in the hurricane's eye
then I will turn to salt without looking back
as the wave smashes itself to foam

if we are ciphers spelling ethereal blessings
then we are shadows echoing whispers
as we sift our shameless hands through virtue's dust

Critique

Let's go down by the river
and light its oil slick on fire.
On its bank of slag and tar
I will set out a meal for you
atop a cloth of Kevlar.
Salad of goldfish
with eucalyptus leaves
and plasma dressing—
never mind the tiny eyes.
Never mind if they said
your poem sucks—
after my own mother
wanting me dead,
I'd take it as rough praise.
I'll wear my holographic gown
for you—down to a nub.
We'll consummate our meal
beside the insoluble river.
It smells like radium,
the sizzling light.
Here, have more goldfish.

The Plumbing on Oak Street

Unit 4 colludes with Unit 5 to remove
the dark neighbors and install lighter ones.
Housekeeper holds sign to window: *Llame Policía.*
Pipe drips rust into subterranean garage.

Nice law student in Unit 6 floats in her trust-fund
bubble above her husband's kitchen drug business,
the kids always with breakfast in their hair.
Dark trickles from front gate to apartment door.

Newlyweds in Unit 3 always flash the oversize
flat-screen, the Infiniti, the Dolce Gabbana,
nasty gossip following their big white hellos.
In Unit 2, the ceiling light is hemorrhaging.

Unit 1, absentee owners, seven years behind
on the regime, pay the judgment upon sale—
to a family from the Moonie Wedding.
Upstairs, the tub is filling from the drain.

The child in Unit 2 screams constantly,
interesting the authorities, in turn causing strife
with Unit 6. A breadcrumb trail shows the way.
Plumber says *Lady—for this you need a priest.*

The Jezebel Retires

What rain is raining ghosts tonight, what arms
have lain—go back to Edna's *Odes to Slaves*.
Once-treasured names, recede into the waves,
take your damn faces with! It was the norm,
you say? More like, any port in a storm.
A certain summer sang in me, alright,
a fire keeping lovers hot all night—
noon's ashen quiet, the ignored alarm.
Let it rain all winter, is what I say.
Let fake love's flotsam lodge on this cold
beach-head, let the soft seed in the hard shell
snatch at its chance and sprout. Single and old,
palm trees stand tall on the shore and sway
serenely in the breeze, roots fast in Hell.

Dream Date

Day paints her nails red before slipping on
first one black fishnet stocking, then the other.
She has a lot on her mind.
Desert wind teases her cloud hair.
Sunlight is the slip beneath her hem,
her music the baying of wolves.
Taste of moon on her lips,
with morning dew she perfumes her wrist.
Her finish is so close, she can hear evening
on the treetops through her fingertips.
Now that she's ready, she decides
that King Chango's in Peach Springs,
Arizona, is the place to go—
but she isn't ready, she'll never be ready.
The trucker, hauling trees,
can see that even from a distance
as he approaches her hitch-hiking the Ten in Walnut—
he's seen lot lizards
looking better put-together than that—
Now that dog don't hunt! he mutters
into the CB radio to no-one.
She looks like one of those days
that start out perfectly fine
but then grind to a halt when you floor it.
She's made up her face in the wrong mirror—
the classical mirror of introspection—
while in his rear-view he sees nothing,
not even what is behind him on the road.
Eighty yards up ahead, Day
has her thumb out as she practices
the rhumba along the center divider,
and the trucker reaches his arm out the window,

scooping her up by the waist
at eighty miles an hour
with both hands still on the wheel.
What a vision she is as she tells him
all the things she's seen,
all the people she's been!
The Druid who had been dancing with her
just after dawn back on Le Presqu'Île de Quiberon
showers mistletoe onto the late-model Volvo sleeper.
Poor dumb trucker, he muses,
will be dancing on the head of a pin,
talking nonsense
with his arms around a beautiful cadaver,
once the stars' heavy shadows finish her off.
And there we see him, his truck over the side,
trees and midnight scattered everywhere,
his tears wetting the match
as he laughs with the Druid over a cigarette,
wondering who she was and where she went.
<<C'est la guerre>>,
the CB radio reminds them in English
—only the radio is off—
the tractor is on its side in the woods,
and Day dimished
to a scarlet fingernail of moon low in the west.

III.

On the Wing

Migration

                    I've
                heard it's
            pretty, this
          paved-over swamp.
        I ask you: stinging
      gnats, kudzu-enshrouded
         dogwoods, blue laws, debutantes,
            hundreds of miles between paintings,
               yellow-dawg conservatives, sewer
            stench befouling stagnant air? —What about
              the Ventura Freeway in August
           at four miles an hour, the morning
         toxicity forecast, art
        shows where we look for our-
      selves in the glass, beach-
    impetigo,
     and earthquakes?
    you ask
      me.
        —Ninety
          museums,
       Venice Boardwalk,
           the Flower District,
             eighty-six languages,
           Korean soap operas,
       Malibu dissolving into
    red Pacific sunsets, that right at
Topanga, Tom Waits at the Pantages,
   need I go further? —Sawhorse tables,
       bonfires, old surfers telling tales
       in raunchy Gaelic fashion
      over beer and oysters
     we gathered beside
   herons fishing
  the rank shoals
   of Mad
Creek.

Moon Shell

Grandmother-breast, blue-veined dun, moon shell.
Fiddle-head, cyclone, galacticized skeleton, moon shell.

Sand washed underfoot spills out, spills in.
Rock-hard water, calculus of carbon, moon shell.

Light-rays divide and spin through channels of bone.
Shadowy eye of whale, of Edisto Indian, moon shell.

Caress of crab-claw and whelk, of mountain stone.
Futility lunges at muscular ocean, moon shell.

Are dolphins' whistles etched in the growth-rings?
No—oceans mirrored in the ears of children, moon shell.

The Druid shifts it hand-to-hand: eternal spiral/failed circle?
Christening-gown, fortress, bungalow, coffin, moon shell.

April Pacific

How beautiful, the stars
above the empty coast
shining in his mother's hair.
Red poppies stain

night's empty coast
beside the dirt road.
Red poppies brush
a white shawl fluttering

in a dirt road
in slow chilly air.
Her white shawl flutters,
her eyes cloud over.

Slow chilly air
stirs the madroñas.
Her eyes cloud over
under Scorpio's moon.

Nothing stirs but madroñas,
poppies, and stars.
Scorpio's moon wanders
the scaffolded sky

between poppies and stars,
shining in his mother's hair.
Scaffolding the sky,
how beautiful, the stars.

The Devil Cruises PCH

His high-fired hoof prints sgraffito the mud
where he pulled over on the blind curve
six miles back, to take a leak in the sage.
All you doubters, go and look.
Put your fingers in the wounded earth.
You don't hear the acrid eggs in your mouth?
The Devil's fifty-nine Chevy convertible
has a bad muffler and a headlight out, and stickers
reading *Beam Me Up Scotty* and *Kill Your TV.*
The travelers he's after don't thumb rides.
He wants the ones stuck in the house,
sick of keeping their crayons inside the lines,
whose crayons move without their hands,
whose hands fashion shadow puppets
while their crayons conceive purple children.
Human frailty, he muses, could be summed up
by the Heisenberg Uncertainty Principle.
The Devil has a wild love for the broken world.
He cranks the AM radio up loud
when the tuner hits *You Light Up My Life*.
Baptists look so trashy, trying not to dance.
He's an iambic dancer, nimble hoof and club foot.
The Devil's face turns wistful, almost tender,
in the dashboard's greenish light
as he ponders asking God for a reconciliation.
He closes his eyes and prays, *Dear God,*
see that Four-eyes up at the ramp?
What if I bring her to your place instead of mine?
How about we exchange a few pleasantries
over a burnt offering. I'd be glad to pick up
a little blood on the way over. Amen.

He envisions a future his old nemesis can't imagine,
given the prophesies and all:
the Devil will repent, God will repent,
and they'll move back in with Mary and Jesus,
and work out their differences. Looking
for a clearer radio station, the Devil
runs his heap off the road. Back at the curve,
his ceramic hoof prints fill with rain.

God Devil Ghazal

So God makes up with the Devil as an example for the mortals.
Their tour starts with an Alabama casino, among the mortals.

God wants to see the Hollywood Wax Museum. Satan demurs:
Who needs a wax Monroe among the mortals?

In Dublin, Lucifer suggests a talk at Trinity on the Book of Kells.
Rugby, says God. *Redneck,* mutters El Diablo, among the mortals.

In Samaria the Enemies recall the polygamist and Jesus at the well.
Rampant, admires Beelzebub, *thy gift of libido, among the mortals.*

God and the Devil fight over a woman in a Warsaw laundromat.
It's her boring outfit that saves her soul, among the mortals.

In Florence, Lucifer notices the fortunes bestowed on the Church.
The irony is lost on God, polishing his halo among the mortals.

Old Scratch wants to see how his famine is going in Sudan.
God jets off to prayers in Morocco, among the mortals.

In Beijing, God shoves Satan in the pool to see if he'll sizzle.
Satan thrashes and chokes, and gets a zero among the mortals.

God invites The Incubus to a dry wedding at Stockholm Cathedral.
Asmodius tells him, *Revelry is the way to go among the mortals.*

The Evil One asks God to Sotheby's but God is too broke to go.
Satan acquires *Discobolos* and a large Rothko among the mortals.

Satan, shivering in Moscow, wants to go yachting off Krakatoa.
Clever God agrees, and whips up a cyclone among the mortals.

In Paris, Mephistopheles orders his winter wardrobe at McQueen.
God hears his nemesis advise a gigolo among the mortals.

The Devil yawns. God says it's time He went on back up the hill.
All they can agree on is, next time fly solo among the mortals.

Satan lingers to watch an artist having a go at his neighbor's wife.
There's a right way to nibble La Araña's toes, among the mortals.

Whisper, Ashes, Night

In the taxi home your date whispers,
cinder-voiced, *Never mind the ashes,*
we won't be needing any stars tonight.

But tonight there's not going to be any night.
Orange haze billows pungent whispers,
And at your gate, cinders hiss, becoming ashes.

Hellish odor, burnt breath of ashes:
your loom, the Rothko, Mom's papers. Tonight
no difference between scream and whisper.

Darkness-gone-solid reddening your eyes, whisper
dragon, icarus, phoenix into the ashes,
proceed into illuminated night.

Ode on Red

> *dragging his body behind him like a wet mattress*
> —Anne Carson

That last red rim of Helios dropping
Into the wine-dark sea below the Palisades
Thrilled him like original sin

As did sharing a slice
Of one of Geryon's herd—
Here, watch it bleed when you stick it—

Closing night of the big Viola Retrospective,
He thought it was supposed to be Bach,
Not glorified loft-videos—ditched that—

Took her to the Good Luck for a cosmo
Whole joint upholstered in Red he said *My
Favorite* compassing her in his mind like suede

His paintings were red his rug was red
The traffic light on his corner, only ever red
He put on *Kind of Blue* to throw her off a little

The walls nearly bled as he poured
Three fingers of Añejo into a ruby
Tumbler closed his eyes and began

The Red Terrance

Let's just say all Art has broke loose
and is booking it down the court
three times faster than the visitors,
and if he wants to preside a dreadlocked
or mohawked seven-foot
over the ivory tower, then So be it.
His third eye butterflies the red tide,
never mind *Go Cocks* tail-gaters
or their simpleton brothers,
who haven't a notion what thumbnail moon
gave rise to Dizzy or James Brown or Himself.
Decay loves Suffragette the way
Anagram loves Strom's black daughter.
Say you'd seen the letterman discreetly
refuse a beauty from across the table.
Postmodern, yes, and righteous,
but also, darkness waits in the vacant desert
for a mad sun to rise.
I miss my wife, I miss my kids,
is his lament, as poets of every station
follow from dry creek bed to parachute
that wind, rattling its bones in a box.

Blueaille

after Joseph Cornell

Brilliant, how you lure cotingas into the shabby
seaside lodgings of your untraveled memory:
in their cages, fashion operettas of the mundane.

libretti   bubble pipes   cat-bones   compasses

Of the life devoted to your invalid brother,
make a world of ten thousand exquisite things.
Be the Ulysses of the tethered ankle.

ticket stubs   indigo silk   paper birds   telescope-lenses

Let others found their dynasties, paint portraits
in lapis: yours will be the seeds
falling on the bluest peninsulas.

French menus   oaken spheres   mouse fuzz   gyroscopes

Let your grimy little street's smoggy days
turn cerulean, and your moonless nights'
wild auroras burn green and purple.

lithographed children   mirrors   butterflies   piston rings

Your room will be the most artful nook on the Seine,
your companions the physicists and ballerinas
of Europe, your conversations the most daring.

balsa propellers   goblets   seashells   DC circuits

We can almost hear the music box's tiny marimba,
the pop and hiss of vinyl enshrining a tenor
in a cobalt enamel gramophone.

glass actresses   Codd marbles   feathers   clock-springs

When the future crowds around
your impeccably dilapidated steamer trunk,
blue light will emanate as it yawns open.

Blueaille, you called it.

Spectrophotometry

Morning dew on centipede grass glitters
like a broken windshield in the street,
like glass chips fixed in the stucco

of a remote Oaxacan village. The fifth
tornado bulletin this week
interrupts more bad economic news.

Prismatic in the sun, the whole village
is bathed in red, then green, finally purple.
God is revealed in a young surfer who lost

her arm to a monster she calls her sharky, as in,
the day my sharky gave me a new challenge.
Clocks gather dust on hardware shelves:

locals use the changing colors to tell time.
Another school shooting, today in Charlotte.
My friend, who started The Three-Meter Bridge

Walk, across palm fronds laid over a ditch
at low tide, has taken his life. Not a break
in the geometry of space, but an arc

in the continuum of time. Shall we drink oil
when the water runs dry? Meet me at the *zócalo*
for coffee, *Chulita,* when the hour is turquoise.

After Many Years Out West

A man comes in the store where she cashiers.
She asks herself if that could be the boy
she had once tried to love in her inept way.
Prosperous, married, greying and now short-haired,
handsome as ever, even deeper-voiced.
How many years ago now, thirty-three?
They loved, and failed, each other utterly—
the way wild children will, more urge than choice—
in a matter of twelve weeks. Now in the store
where she moonlights, a greying person gives
his credit card. She the buoyant, licentious,
unwanted teen, he with the madonna/whore
thing. She smiles as she hands him his purchase
and says, *We're glad you shopped today with us.*

Leave

for Holaday

Leave Venice now, its atmosphere of ozone
and Xanax, its architecture of crack and tinsel,
stride like Santiago Burn across the desert
to the trochaic meter of your inner clock.
Flights are cheap, the heat has fractured,
the waves are running in sonnets out of the south.
Leave in your green velvet pumps
and your rhinestone wig,
with your silk hem trailing sparks,
your head on fire and your tongue on fire.
Leave your vagrants, your yoga-ninnies and cineastes.
Come with new drafts and a fifth of Campari,
wearing that slight censorious frown.
Today, facts and trawlers sparkle at the surface:
Charleston is awash in self-deception.
Above bad movies and their consequences,
in spite of shadows roiling inside your head,
if not flying, then by whatever means at hand.
For whom our insipid museum should acquire
the collected works of Lucien Freud,
for whom our mayor would devour the Decameron,
for whom the Citadel cadets ought parade in anapests—
boys on tall ships are lining the yardarms in salute.
We can hold hands and scream bloody murder.
We can eat contraband creek shrimp and Vicodin,
drink raw oysters steeped in white lightning.
I can show you houses in glory and in decay,
show you pelicans above and dolphins below
our seven black rivers that flash
their bright inscriptions through the dark.
I can present you at the court of Queen Skreet.

Everyone will lose their illusions
and look for better ones, compose
bagpipe threnodies on your divorce,
bring you collages of sweet-grass and shark's blood.
Come you, like Shoemaker-Levy, blasting above
those seven bridges, high across the marsh,
before a long inscrutable streak of words,
from Venice, over the Cadillac Ranch,
across the hollowed-out eye of New Orleans—
this very minute, leave.

Pythia Barbara

Ninety-six in the shade, the last errand
of the day, *I was a free man*

in Paris bursts from the window next to hers
as she loads her sacks into the car,

kiwi fruit, baby spinach, sourdough
baguette, pomegranate, prosciutto—

lately their restaurant bill has gotten
entirely out-of-hand. Now a bulletin

cuts to Hartsfield International, crash
of a Delta communter out of CHS—

Or maybe the song was *Amelia, it
was just a false alarm.* At the red

light, in front of her car,
yellow butterflies catch fire.

Aiken is pure Americana,
she thinks—why bother flying to Atlanta,

it takes less time driving curvy two-lane
roads from here. The last bag rips, being

carried inside. Oranges from Mexico
scorch fingertips, rolling from hand to bowl.

Soapy dishwater smells of burning wires.
The souls of the passengers mingle and rise

to heaven on ink-black smoke.
The refrigerator crackles and sparks.

White ashes smelling of singed hair
descend upon the sacred Chattahoochee River.

Charon meets them at peak adrenalin,
is how the poem will come to be written.

She inhales chicken simmering with celery, kale,
and thyme. Friendly Charon is texting for help,

and the flight crew feels safe now, as he lands
his boat at the river's edge, extends his hand.

No-one

They are calling Zone 1. I approach the uniformed agent and say, *I have no seat.* She asks if I have a bar code. Yes. *Your seat has already been assigned. When you go through, you'll be told what it is.* I go through. I put my palm on the laser. 28B, another uniformed agent tells me. Twenty-eight Bee. I take my seat in a row of three, between no-one. A woman in a batik caftan takes the window seat. I wince at the coffee-stain on my t-shirt. A man wearing business-casual takes the aisle seat, but then moves elsewhere. The woman tells me, *I raised my grandchild.* I reply, *I raised no-one, and no-one raised me.* The plane begins to taxi. She looks at me with her eyes, *Tell me that again, this time with love.* The man who is not there leans towards us to listen.

Pura Vida

Looks pretty gnarly and we're old and out-of-shape,
but he and I hit the water anyhow—hell, we came all this way.
The sun blazes. It's the Devil's own bathtub.
Sharks smell the chaos; stingrays hover, poised to dart.
Pelicans squadron the surface, scanning for prey.
Small deadly jellyfish have all magnetoed shoreward,
where the tarantula and centipede creep, and the *congo* howls.
Gin-clear shallows part easily under our hands.
Olivine kelp-beds sway, rooted to basalt pillows below.
I am all grom again, that sweet fire-wet dazzle.
The foam is head-high, lightning-white, tastes like metal.
He powers forward, punches the nose under the soup.
I never learned to do that, and I get blendered.
This is the Pacific, after all, bright hammer of *matanzas*.
So I gather myself and let the violent sun beat down.
He kicks out of a closing section and prones toward me,
taking my hand—somehow this helps me paddle better.
The waves soon lull and we both make it outside
to calm unbroken seas, and we wait for the next set,
bailing tides of gossip out of our fetched-up lives.
Making it out is one thing. It's the getting back in.
A set emerges, dark, friendly, and utterly without mind.
I watch him stroke into a peak and set his line,
launching an aerial into the clouds, and out of sight.
Though spent, I angle into the next wave. As I plant my feet
and unfold my body, the bowl vaporizes under me.
I'm ragdolled in the trough, the lip smashing my board in half.
¡Puta mierda, que desmadre! I body in on a broken wave.
Down the line, his board smashes against lava rocks.
Its shadow flutters on the bright sand below.
From far above the deafening clouds, he calls my name.

Crossing

Stripping my life of comforts, I begin. One cotton shift,
no shoes. Sleep on the ground, eat black bread, drink water.

At sunrise, I kneel in the clearing to pray.
I wear a knotted cord around my head to signify.

My chores, my only break from prayer. I do what Mama says
and come straight back. My cord says, *No talking to this one.*

Alone in the wild with The Spirit and The Book
I dream only God and the Ones who lead me toward Him.

Bare feet, cotton shift, black bread. I find a rough pine
branch to talk to. My echoes sing me The Book, The Light.

O, my guide, be revealed to me. I am alone, but not alone.
See me along my journey. See into my dreams.

*My child, do you not green with? So firey and waving,
so time. Where we eclipse, never fall sweet.*

So speaks my guide, and I understand. Heron-track,
white-tail buck speak also. Rough stick, black water.

I do not cross until I have my name. When the bright image.
Who will know me, once I have been given my dream?

I was girl. I am not a girl. I do not know what I am.
I walk into the river. The song, the book, the light.

The Shot

The puppy I just watched get run over and I go check the garden to see if the lettuce has sprouted yet. She sniffs at the dirt and says *Nope—another day or two.* We grab one end of a stick and Louie chomps the other for tug-o-war. With the puppy who lit out from under the vintage Indian bike on a crushed leg, I go check the mail. No mail. She runs circles around me back towards my house. At her house there's nobody home. She is at the shelter getting morphine and her squashed belly assessed by a vet, and commences to dig a hole near my trash can. I ask her if she is afraid or lonely, and she says to throw her the ball. She says to let her in bed with me, because there's snow on the ground. She laps up a big drink of water with her fast little tongue and wonders if the guy on the bike is okay. *Well, he's pretty mad but he'll get over it. Some scrape on his helmet,* I tell her, *You don't mess around.* We sit on the sofa watching *Making It Grow*. I rub her face, so ugly it's cute. She says she's just got to chase bikes, it's a genetic thing. At the shelter the vet gives her the shot. As I weed the collards I hold her in my lap, gently, because she's so badly damaged. Drowsy, she licks the earthy sweat of my hand.

Jubilate Louie

For though by nature vigilant and protective,
yet he is easily approached in friendship.
For, born of the tribe of Ridgeback,
the great Lion-Hunters of mighty Africa,
he will give chase to all manner of creature.

For his antibiotic tongue relieves all manner of sore.
Nor does he bark overly, and neither does he slobber,
unlike the fancy and expensive boxer,
given to course the yard, over the shouts and curses
of the mighty landlord, and thence to thrust
its pendulous flews into one's crotch,
leaving ropes of drool upon one's bare summer leg.

For the snout of Louie is pointy, like that of a hound,
and his ears flop over, handsomely and expressively so,
and are made exquisitely keen, and as velvet to the touch.
For he can raise them in anticipation,
or lower them in disappointment.

For when he gallops across the meadow at Idyllwild,
'tis as if t'were his first time in an open field,
and he leaps as in the Jules Feiffer dance,
and his ears flap as do flap the wings of Gabriel.
For he is a fastidious creature and well-groomed,
his four white socks shine good as new,
and his kohl eyeliner accentuates and defines as Maybelline.
For thus could I follow his example more closely.

For he is a careful eater, sniffing every morsel offered.
For his bark is of a pleasant baritone timbre,
and serves admirably as our doorbell—
else be it the pizza man, always presented
with the curious ears and helicopter tail.

For although unmanageable by nature,
he does always strive to please when shewn a crust of bread,
which, of all the foods of man, gives him greatest delight,
as when he did drag his master fully four city blocks
for the want of a most wastefully discarded sack of bagels.

For he is variously communicative, marshalling all of his parts:
for joy, he gets righteous air, all four paws aloft.
for fear, he bolts running as he never otherwise runs,
and bounds for his master's shelter.
For in anger he leaps onto the bed, and with his snout,
tosses covers and pillows and makes a great pandemonium.
For adoration, he croons pleasantries with his doggy growl.
For in refusal to enter the public outhouse,
he does wrinkle his face and plant his four legs
well away from the door in a grand shew of canine disgust.

For he is the ablest of sentinels,
and when he refuses to enter the park,
we know Here Be Alligators.
For if, at three o'clock in the morning,
he should stand on the bed between us,
next shall we hear a mighty thunder from heaven.
For he always chooses the foot of our bed,
likewise the door of the tent, for sleeping.

For he likes all dogs generally,
and certain bitches especially. For he is finder
of lost dogs, and defender of imperiled dogs,
as the time he came upon his dachshund friend Sophie
being stalked by a pitbull, and attacked the miscreant,
to the fullest astonishment of all who knew him—

then wrangled himself out of its jaws and seized
upon the monster's neck, until the owner
did come in haste, and with manifest apology.

For his love of Mobalie, the young terrier
who adored him likewise, and for his grief
at the loss of her beneath the vintage Indian bike.
For his own short life, that reminds me how short
is my own—for that he lives in the moment,
and in the absolute security of the moment.
For his love is unconditional, and spiritual, and joyful.

For never would he dip his toe in the dog lake,
even in fiercest heat, and as he watched
the multitude of dogs frolic and swim therein,
'twere as though they had devils cast into them.
Until the day whereupon he galloped into the waters
after his ball, and, feeling the lake floor drop—
but being in the Spirit—Louie continued to run,
and swam, and knew that he was swimming.

On the Wing

after Sister Gertrude Morgan

All kinds of creatures in Heaven's bestiary.
They protect my labors from the Tokoloshe.
Sometimes the innocents follow Satan's black poodle.
The words at the beginning are also at the end.

Red jaguar plays tug-o'-war with a purple lamb.
Chartreuse gargoyle grooms yellow jackalope.
Dragons witness their orangeness cast into the earth.
All kinds of colors in Heaven's bestiary.

Spectral fishes neon through bright bluey jello.
Heaven's stone gargoyles hover with hummingbirds.
Heaven's dogs dream *Behold! God Army.*
They protect my labors from the Tokoloshe.

Teal dogs paddle after holy kayaks in Heaven's red lake.
They inspire all dogs on earth to sainthood—
except my dogs, suffered nevermore to visit Dog Lake,
since the innocents follow Satan's black poodle

right on across. Heaven's dogs dream *Behold! God Army.*
Holy Ghost Power swims them away to freedom.
I stand on the bank of the lake, calling and calling,
and my words when I start are the same when I'm done.

I've got four now on the wing in Heaven's bestiary.
Edna, Sully, Moe, and Louie protect me from the Tokoloshe.
Forever into temptation they follow Satan's black poodle,
and the word at the beginning is the word at the end.

A Poet Takes His Girl Dancing

The fastest substance in the universe is light,
at times less stuff than circumstance—
although it is the stuff my other hands
are made of, when they aren't made of glass.
Your dress was cool and silky to the touch,
as I waltzed you through that plate-glass window,
more light than substance. Bloody hands and elbows,
but we didn't care so much, since we're not much
but carbon, gas, a circumstantial spark.
By night, plate-glass is blacker than your dress,
but not by much. I always have loved glass,
loved you—cool, transparent in the dark—
The slowest light, cool, black in our hands, sublime,
as we broke through together, that last time.

Four Different Kinds of Light

A hurricane lamp-glow, throwing a yellow stain over a greasy smear of time on the slanted ceiling, reveals a crack in the language. The filthy orange of a street light elbows rudely past the half moon. Bluish light fluoresces down from a warehouse utility fixture onto you, in white linen, tipping your hat. *He is not real,* I tell myself. The lamplight flickers, disturbed by my song as I stand in my dead sister's boots. I'm trying to be late for my wake. The flames remind me that it is foolish to go to your own wake—even if you are lucid along the way.

Notes

"Alkahest"—a bouts-rimés sonnet.

"April Pacific" borrows a line from "Mi Mamá, the Playgirl," by Richard Garcia.

"Chicken Theory"—a substitution poem; also a concrete poem in which the stanza shape mimics that of William Carlos Williams's stanza in "The Red Wheelbarrow".

"Crossing"—a redaction poem, modified from two oral accounts of the Gullah-Geechee ritual of passage into adulthood, called "Seeking." The author regrets that the precise online sources can no longer be found.

"The Devil Cruises PCH"—a Twenty Little Poetry Projects ("Simmerman") poem, devised by Jim Simmerman. Pacific Coast Highway (PCH), CA-1, skirts the California coast from Dana Point to Mendocino. *Sgraffito* is graffiti scratched, rather than inked, into a surface.

"Dream Date"—a Simmerman poem.

"Jubilate Louie"—after a fragment of Christopher Smart's 18th century poem, *Jubilate Agno,* praising the poet's cat, Jeoffry.

"Killer King"—"Red side" refers to an emergency room's surgical crew, as opposed to its medical "blue side." O'Keeffe and Merritt is a mid-century cook-stove popular in Southern California. "Gomer" is a pejorative coined by Samuel Shem, M.D.

"Kyoto Protocol"—a haiku acrostic.

"On the Wing"—a cascade. Tokoloshe (pronounced TokoLOSsee) is a capricious Zulu water-sprite: a jinx. "Behold! God Army" comes from a bygone Charleston mural by Rev. Robert Parks.

"Prussian Model"—a bouts-rimés sonnet, titled after a militaristic teaching method aimed at fulfilling the modern state's aim of cheap, minimal, compulsory mass education, adopted throughout the United States by 1900.

"Pythia Barbara"—the pythia revealed the future to the ancient Greeks by going into a smoke-induced trance. The poem is in slant-rhymed couplets.

"Sand, Glass, Moon"—a tritina, namely, half a sestina.

"Sonnet Comparing Two David Lehmans"—a bouts-rimés on the end-words from W. H. Auden, "In The Time Of War, Xii."

"Termite Art"—a term coined by film critic Manny Farber referring to the earnest aesthetic drive of B-movies.

"Zeitgeist"—a double abecedarian, devised by Barbara Hamby.

About the Author

Katherine Williams is a white Southerner who grew up in the military, mostly in Virginia, California, and South Carolina. She has published four chap books and read at venues from the L.A. Arts District to the College of Charleston. The Pushcart nominee's poems appear in *Spillway, Projector, Diagram, Measure, SC Review,* and elsewhere. A UCLA biomedical research technician, she moved back home to James Island, SC, twenty years ago with poet Richard Garcia.

There she continued in biomedicine, and with Richard established the Long Table Poets, an ongoing workshop for study, writing, and critique. Writing poetry centers her, and helps her think more deeply; her calling came in 1991, the day after attending a reading with Luis Alfaro at Self Help Graphics in East L.A. and witnessing the energy poetry could create among strangers.

Williams is a community arts advocate who produced occasional readings in Los Angeles, spearheaded the James Island Arts Council, and founded Poetry at McLeod, a series in which illustrious Black poets present their art at a Southern cotton plantation now dedicated to researching and honoring the lives of people who were enslaved there. Her hobbies include surfing, art, politics, playing the cello, fixing computers, and homemaking.

www.ingramcontent.com/pod-product-compliance
Lightning Source LLC
Chambersburg PA
CBHW030051170426
43197CB00010B/1480